150 MANDALAS

— ADULT COLORING BOOK —

VOLUME 2

Studio Ant Press

150 MANDALAS Adult Coloring Book (Volume 2)
by Studio Art Press

© Copyright 2023 by Studio Art Press

All rights reserved.

We hope you will enjoy our book! As a small start-up company, your feedback is very important to us. Please feel free to leave a review of our book, this will really help us understand if we did a good job!

This Book Belongs To:

_____

Studio Art Press

The Preview Page:

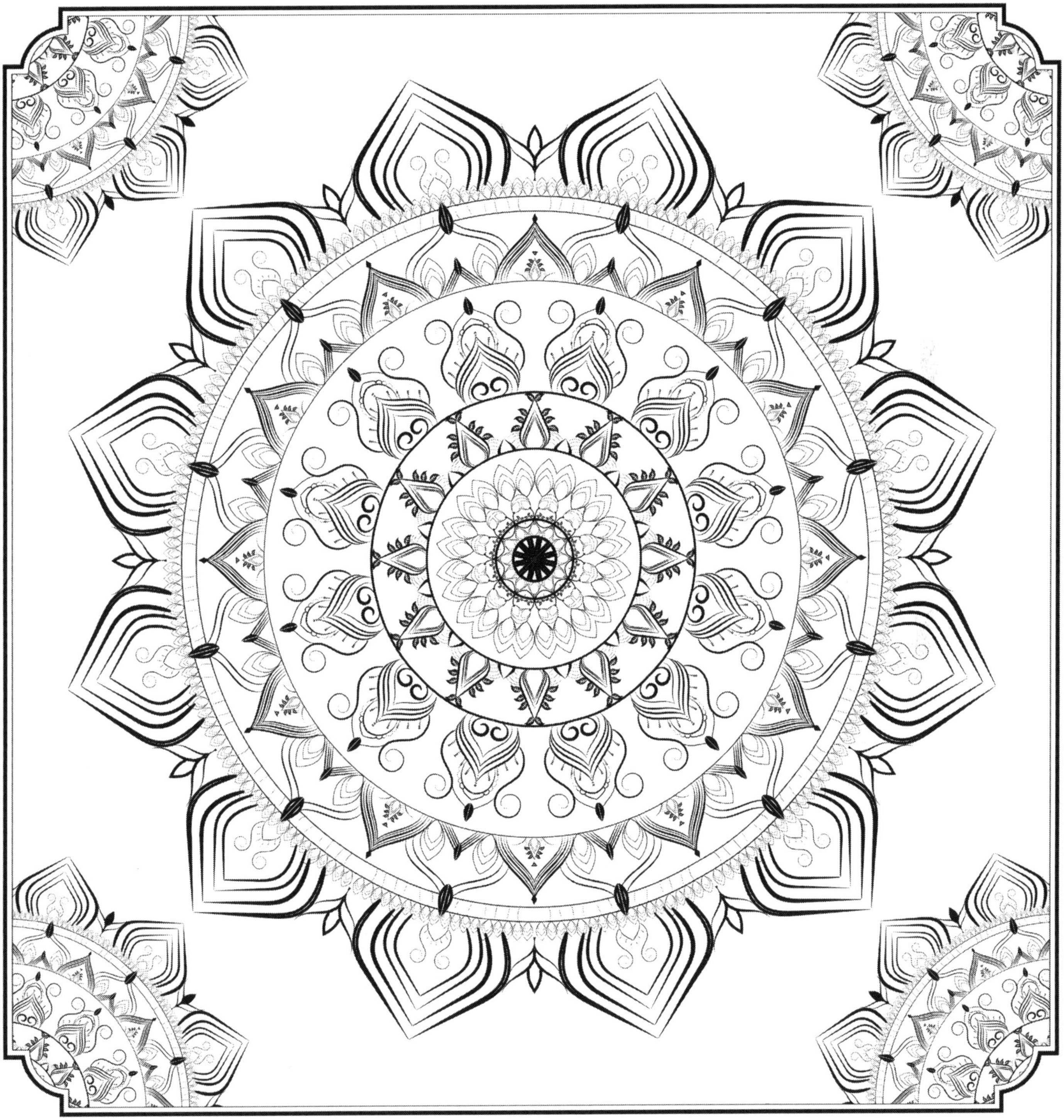

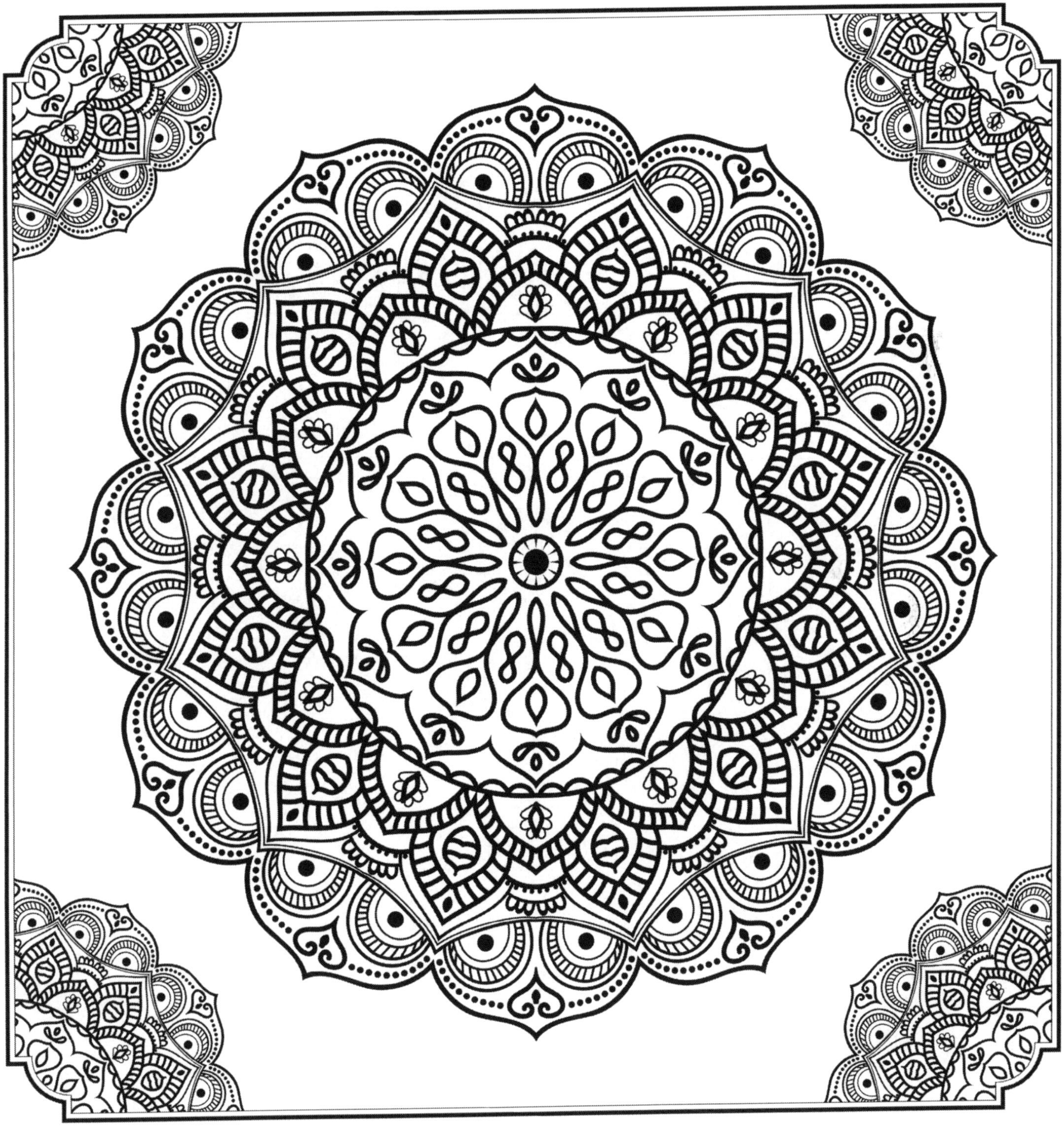

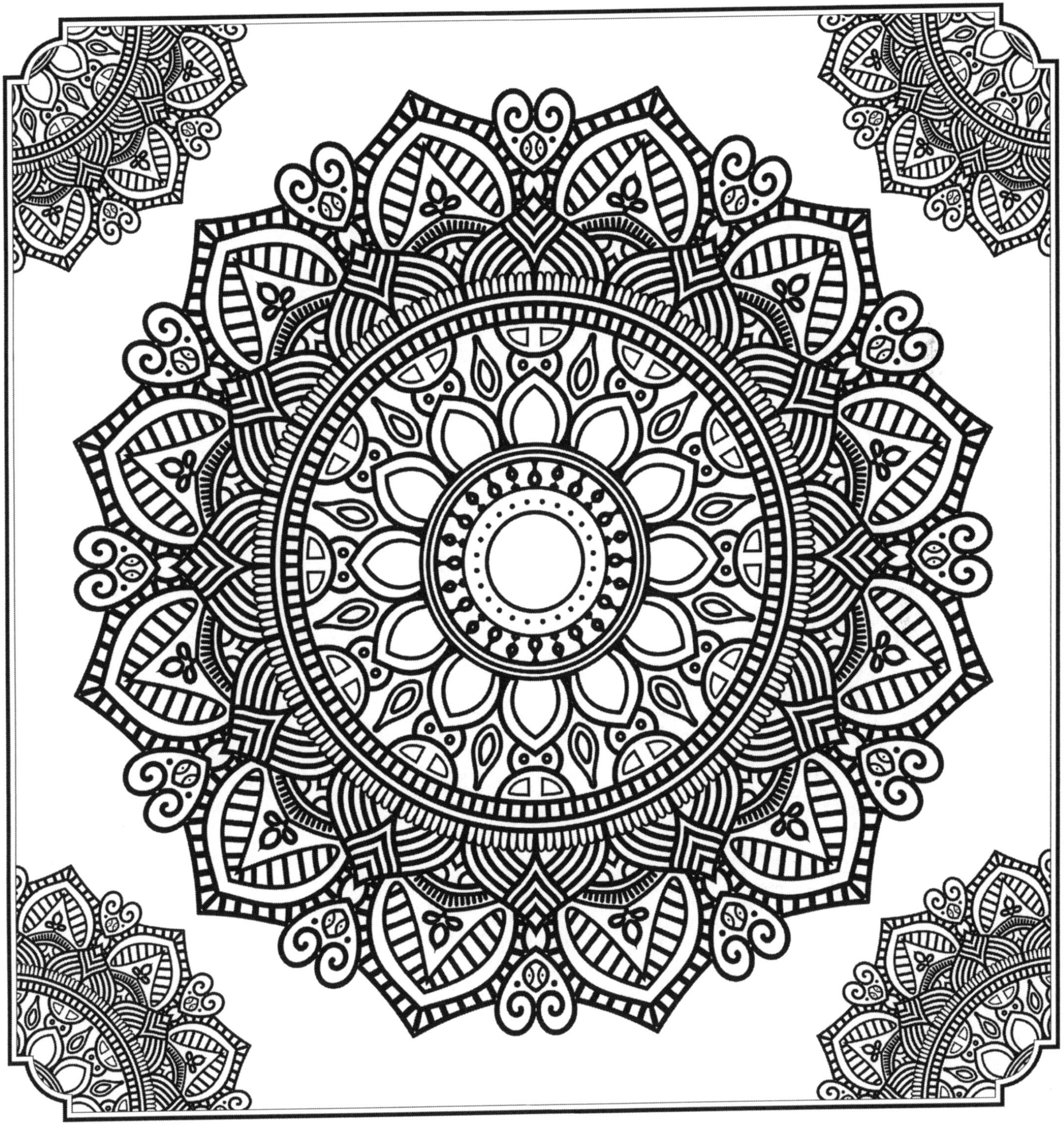

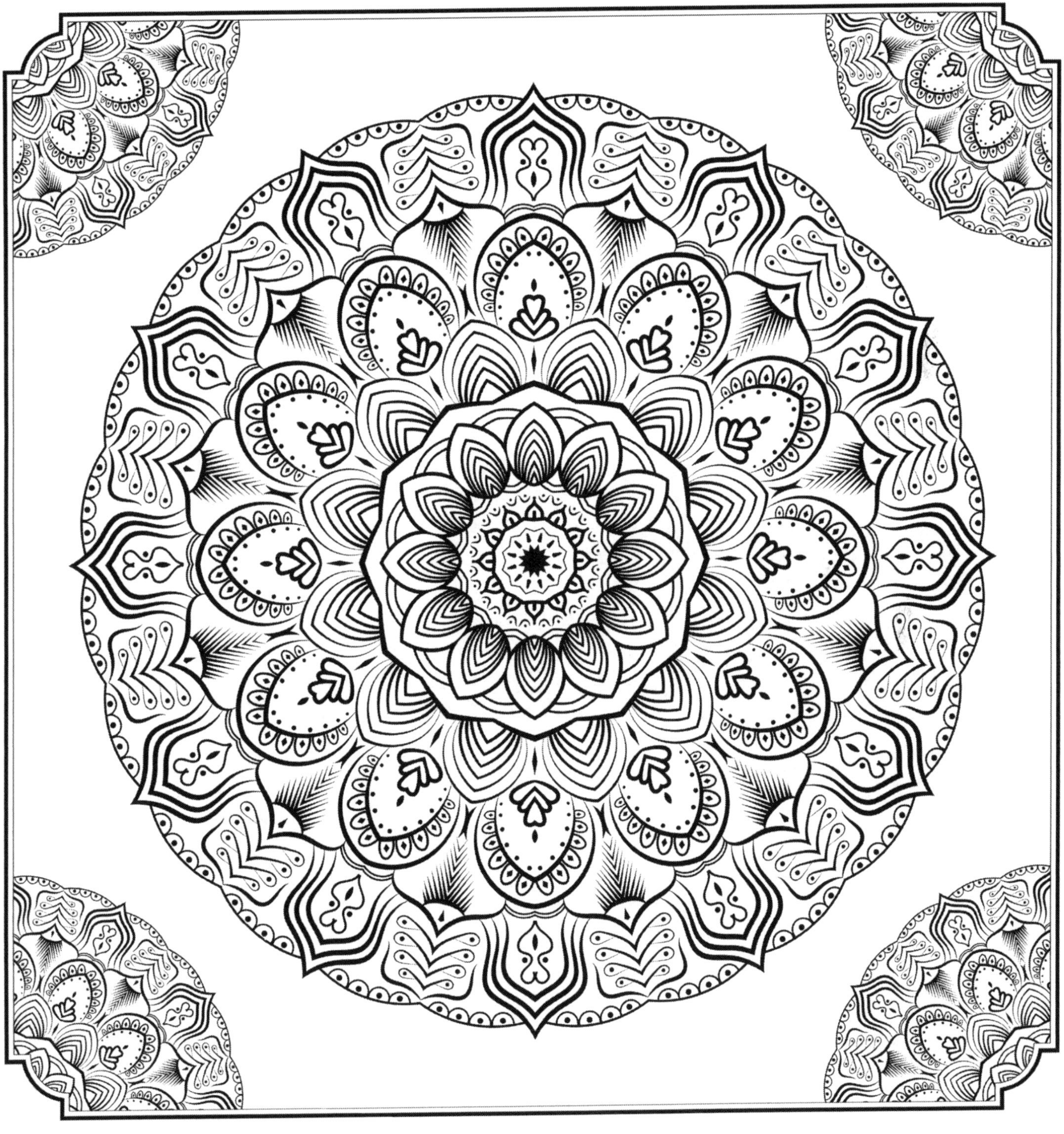

Thank You So Much For Purchasing this Book!

We hope you enjoyed our book.

As a small start-up company, your feedback is very important to us.

Please feel free to leave a review to our book, this will really help us understand

if we did a good job, or let us know you like it at:

studio.art.press@gmail.com

Olso we have prepared

A GIFT for you!

It is a **digital copy** (PDF) for free,

to print and use it for another member of your family.

To get it, use the camera of your phone to scan the **QR CODE** below.

Scan Me

Studio Art Press

Studio Art Press